Ladybirds

Thea Feldman

KINGFISHER

First published 2015 by Kingfisher
an imprint of Pan Macmillan
a division of Macmillan Publishers Ltd
20 New Wharf Road, London N1 9RR
Associated companies throughout the world
www.panmacmillan.com

Series editor: Polly Goodman
Literacy consultant: Hilary Horton

ISBN: 978-0-7534-3874-9

9 8 7 6 5 4 3 2 1
1TR/0315/WKT/UG/115MA

A CIP catalogue record for this book is available from the British Library.

Printed in China

Picture credits
The Publisher would like to thank the following for permission to reproduce their material.
Top = t; Bottom = b; Centre = c; Left = l; Right = r
Cover Shutterstock/ninii; Pages 3 Shutterstock/chris2766; 4–5 Shutterstock/PHOTO FUN;
5 Naturepl/Rod Williams; 6 Shutterstock/SJ Allen; 7 Shutterstock/Katarina Christenson;
8–9 Nature/Chris Shields (WAC); 10 Shutterstock/PHOTO FUN; 11 Shutterstock/Henrik Larsson;
12–13 Shutterstock/Zigzag Mountain Art; 14–15 Frank Lane Picture Agency (FLPA)/Albert de
Wilde; 15 Naturepl/Doug Wechsler; 16t Shutterstock/PHOTO FUN; 16–17 Shutterstock/Christian
Musat; 18 Flickr/muffinn; 19t Flickr/Gilles San Martin; 19b Flickr/Jean-Daniel Echenard;
20 Naturepl/Doug Wechsler; 21 Shutterstock/PHOTO FUN; 22–23 Naturepl/Rolf Nussbaumer;
24 Naturepl/Rolf Nussbaumer; 25 Naturepl/Nick Upton; 26 Naturepl/Meul/ARCO;
27 Shutterstock/Dimijana; 28 Shutterstock/Steve Shoup; 29t Shutterstock/Arsgera;
29b Shutterstock/Vasca; 30t Shutterstock/trucic; 30b Shutterstock/Christian Musat;
31t Shutterstock/stoupa; 31b Shutterstock/Maria Uspenskaya.

Look at the **insect** on this leaf.

It is a ladybird!

Many ladybirds are red
with black spots.

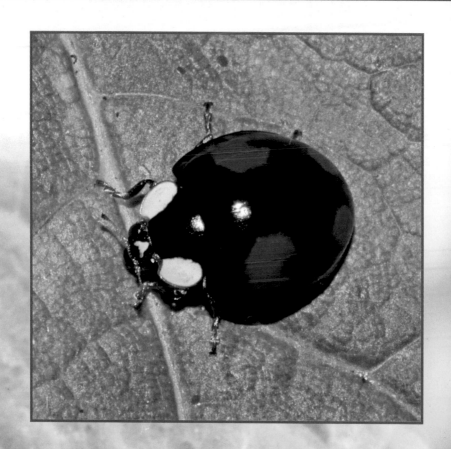

A lot of ladybirds are black with red spots!

Some ladybirds have no
spots at all.

Some ladybirds have stripes!

There are around
5,000 kinds of ladybird.

Most ladybirds have
bright colours.

The colours warn other animals not to eat ladybirds.

Ladybirds have **poison** in them that can make other animals ill.

What do ladybirds eat?
Ladybirds eat **aphids**
(AY-fidz).

Aphids are insects too.

Aphids eat plants in gardens and on farms.

Aphids are not good for plants. People call aphids **pests**.

Not all ladybirds
are female!
There are male
ladybirds too.

male

Most female ladybirds
are a little bigger
than male ones.

female

A female ladybird lays
her eggs on a plant
where aphids live.

Then she leaves.

After four to seven days,
the eggs **hatch**.

A baby ladybird
does not look like
a grown-up ladybird.

A baby ladybird is hungry!

As soon as it hatches,
a baby ladybird starts
to eat aphids.

It can eat 25 aphids a day.

A baby ladybird starts to grow.

It grows so much it becomes too big for its own skin!

The skin splits
open and
falls off.

The ladybird has a new
skin that fits better.

This happens a few times.

When a ladybird is
two or three weeks old,
it holds onto a leaf.

The ladybird's skin splits
open one more time.

Now a hard case covers
the ladybird's body.

After about five more days,
the hard case breaks open.

A grown-up ladybird
comes out.

But it does not
look grown up yet.

A grown-up ladybird comes out with a soft shell.

The soft shell will become hard in a few hours.

The colour of the shell
will change too.

A ladybird's shell
covers its wings.

A ladybird opens its shell
and lifts its wings to fly away!

Where is the ladybird going?

Maybe it is going to eat aphids.

A grown-up ladybird can eat more than 50 aphids a day.

Ladybirds spend the **winter** out of sight in large groups to stay warm.

Ladybirds come out again
when the weather
gets warmer.

When we see ladybirds we know that **spring** is on the way.

Ladybirds will help to take care of plant pests.

Ladybugs have bright colors and are pretty.

Some people say ladybugs bring good luck!

What do you think?

Glossary

aphid a tiny insect that eats plants

hatch to break out of an egg and be born

insect a small animal with six legs

pest an animal that can harm other animals, plants or people

poison something that can make animals ill or even kill them

spring the time of year that comes after winter, when the weather starts to get warmer

winter the coldest time of the year

 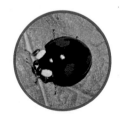